ROMÂNIA

Editions KINA ITALIA

ROMANIA

Surface area: 237,500 km².
Population: 23 million plus about 8 million Romanians living outside the country.

Borders with the Republic of Moldavia to the northeast; with Ukraine to the north and east; with the Black Sea to the southeast; with Bulgaria to the south; with Serbia to the southwest and with Hungary to the west.

Thirty-one percent of the country is covered with mountains and spectacular forests populated by deer, bears, foxes, wild boars, wolves, lynxes, grouse, black goats and many other species of birds. Buffalo, which had totally disappeared, have now been reintroduced to the Carpathians. This is a true oasis in the middle of Europe, a paradise for photography buffs and lovers of the open air. Due to the development of the tourist industry and the traditional hospitality of the Romanian people, the country offers many possibilities in this area.

Thirty-three percent of the country consists of hills and gentle cultivated uplands where numerous marvelous, active monasteries appear as if by magic. The Orthodox monks and pious nuns jealously safeguard the relics of martyred saints.

Thirty-six percent of the country consists of immense fields and broad stretches of land that extend beyond the horizon, sparking the admiration of the farmers from other countries who pass through these areas. Rivers and lakes dot the surface of Romania, which is also traversed by the immense, rich Danube, which forms the border with Serbia and Bulgaria for about 1075 kilometers (almost half of its entire length) and then, before emptying into the Black Sea, creates one of the most important natural areas in the world, the Danube Delta.

Attracted by the splendid beaches, hospitable inns and lively nightlife, every year tourists from all over the world visit the Black Sea coast with its numerous tourist resorts.

One's thoughts return to the ancient Greeks and Romans who reached these lands about 2000 years ago and were enchanted by so much beauty. They added their knowledge and culture to that of the native Dacians as they developed this stupendous land, in the end creating a great people, the Romanians.

Ski resorts, Black Sea bathing areas, thermal healing centers, hotels, international conference centers, entertainment clubs, theaters and religious centers are the principal destinations for the millions of tourists who visit this extraordinary country every year.

RUMÄNIEN

Fläche: 237.500 km2
Einwohner: 23 Millionen und ca. 8 Millionen in der Diaspora.

Es grenzt im Nordosten und im Osten an die Republik Moldawien, im Norden und Osten an die Ukraine, im Südosten an das Schwarze Meer, im Süden an Bulgarien, im Südwesten an Serbien und im Westen an Ungarn.

31% des Gebietes sind von Gebirgen und herrlichen Wäldern bedeckt, in welchen Hirsche, Bären, Füchse, Wildschweine, Wölfe, Luchse, Birkhühner, schwarze Ziegen und zahlreiche Arten von Vögeln leben. In der Karpatengegend ist der Wisent wieder angesiedelt worden, nachdem er bereits ganz verschwunden war. Hier findet man tatsächlich eine wirkliche Oase im Zentrum Europas, ein Paradies für Fotoamateure und Naturliebhaber. Dank der Entwicklung auf dem Touristiksektor und der traditionellen Gastfreundschaft des rumänischen Volkes bietet das Land zahlreiche Möglichkeiten auf diesem Gebiet.

33% des Gebietes besteht aus Hügeln und sanften, bebauten Anhöhen, auf denen sich wie durch ein Wunder die großartigen, noch bewohnten zahlreichen Klöster erheben. In ihnen werden von orthodoxen Mönchen und frommen Nonnen die Reliquien der heiligen Märtyrer mit peinlicher Sorgfalt gehütet.

36% des Gebietes besteht aus Feldern und weiten Flächen, die sich am Horizont verlieren, so groß sind sie. Sie rufen das Staunen der hier vorbeikommenden Landwirte aus anderen Ländern hervor. Flüsse und Seen durchfurchen die Oberfläche Rumäniens, das auch von der unendlich langen, reichen Donau gesäumt wird, die auf eine Länge von etwa 1075 km (fast die Hälfte ihrer gesamten Länge) den Grenzfluß mit Serbien und Bulgarien bildet und eines der wichtigsten naturwissenschaftlichen Gebiete der Welt ist, bevor sie in das Schwarze Meer mündet, nämlich das Donaudelta.

Die Schwarzmeerküste, an der sich die Touristenzentren reihen, ist alljährlich Ziel vieler Besucher aus der ganzen Welt, die von den wunderschönen Stränden, den einladenden Hotels und dem ganz besonders lebhaften Nachtleben angezogen werden.

.....und der Gedanke schweift zu den antiken Griechen und Römern zurück, die vor etwa 2000 Jahren hierher gelangten und von so viel Schönheit bezaubert waren, daß sie ihr Wissen und ihre Kultur zusammen mit der der autochthonen Daker in den Dienst der Entwicklung dieses faszinierenden Landes stellten, bis sie ein großes Volk bildeten, das rumänische Volk.

Skigebiete, Badeorte am Schwarzen Meer, Thermalkurortschaften, Hotels, internationale Kongreßzentren, Unterhaltungslokale, Theater und religiöse Zentren sind die Hauptbezugspunkte für viele Millionen Touristen, die alljährlich dieses außergewöhnliche Land besuchen.

BUCHAREST

The capital of Romania, once known as Little Paris. Today it is more lively than ever, and the city vies for first place as the capital of European culture. Founded in 1459 by prince Vlad Tepeş called Vlad Dracul, a clever politician and fierce warrior, the city of Bucharest derives its name from the shepherd Bucur, which in Rumanian means joy, as good wishes for its future. The city, located in the south-east region of the country, is crossed by the river Dâmboviţa, that runs under the greatest square of the city - Unirii Square. From this square the most important boulevards of Bucharest depart: the most impressive is Unirii Boulevard, that connects Alba Iulia Square to the Parliament Palace, the second largest official building in the world, after the American Pentagon.

BUKAREST

Hauptstadt Rumäniens, seinerzeit auch mit dem Beinamen "Klein Paris". Die Stadt, heute von übersprudelnder Lebhaftigkeit, kandidiert als Hauptstadt der europäischen Kultur. Die Gründung Bukarests im Jahr 1459 war Werk des Prinzen Vlad Tepeş der sich als geschickter Politiker und gefürchteter Kriegsherr auszeichnete und Vlad DRACUL genannt wurde. Der Name der Stadt leitet sich ab von Bucur, dem rumänischen Wort für Freude - als gutes Vorzeichen der Zukunft! Die Stadt liegt im Südosten des Landes und wird vom Fluß Dâmboviţa, durchzogen, der unter ihrem größten Platz - dem Unirii-Platz - herfließt. An diesem Platz nehmen die wichtigsten Boulevards Bukarests ihren Ausgang: Der prächtigste ist der Unirii-Boulevard, der vom Alba Julia-Platz bis zum rumänischen Parlamentspalast führt, dem nach dem amerikanischen Pentagon zweitgrößten Parlamentspalast der Welt.

1 Parliament building and
   International Conference Center
2 I.I.C. Brătianu Hall
3 Parliament Hall
4 Unirii Square
5 13 September entry
6 Parliament building by night

1 Parlamentspalast und
   internationales Kongreßzentrum
2 Saal I.I.C. Brătianu
3 Parlamentssaal
4 Uniriiplatz
5 Eingang 13. September
6 Parlamentspalast bei Nacht

BUCHAREST

The theater, concert and above all opera seasons are the driving forces behind Romanian and international cultural life.

BUKAREST

Die Theater- und Konzertsaisons, besonders aber die Oper, sind Antriebskräfte des rumänischen und internationalen Kulturlebens.

1 *Romanian National Opera House*
2 *The great soprano Gabriela Cegolea, the country's most popular contemporary singer, in the opera Nabucco by Giuseppe Verdi.*
3-4 *Las Bucharest: Casino*
5 *National Theater*
6 *Romanian University*
7 *Triumphal Arch*
8-9 *Dâmboviţa - historic center*

1 *Rumänische Nationaloper*
2 *Die große Sopranistin Gabriela Cegolea, die beliebteste zeitgenössische Nationalsängerin, in der Oper Nabucco von G. Verdi*
3-4 *Las Bucarest: Kasino*
5 *Nationaltheater*
6 *Das rumänische Athenäum*
7 *Triumphbogen*
8-9 *Historisches Zentrum Dâmboviţa*

1 The cathedral of the Romanian Orthodox Patriarchy - Monument from the 17th century, by Constantin Şerban
2 Saint Dimitrius, the patron saint of Bucharest
3 The patriarchal emblem
4 P.F.P. Teoctist, patriarch of the Romanian Orthodox church, along with His Majesty King Michael of Romania upon his return from exile - 1997
5 The outside altar of the patriarchal cathedral

1 Kirche der rumänisch-orthodoxen Patriarchie - Denkmal des XVII. Jh.s. Werk von Constantin Şerban
2 Der hl. Dimitrie, Schutzpatron von Bukarest
3 Das patriarchalische Emblem
4 P.F.P. Teoctist, Patriarch der rumänisch-orthodoxen Kirche, zusammen mit seiner Hoheit König Michael aus Rumänien nach der Rückkehr aus dem Exil - 1997
5 Der äußere Altar der Patriarchalkirche

5

6

7

1 Palace of the Patriarchy
2-3-4-5-7 Details of the Treasury
6 Hall of the Synod

1 Patriarchalkirche
2-3-4-5-7 Details des Schatzes
6 Saal der Synode

Grigore Antipa Natural History Museum

Built in 1834 on order of prince Alessandro Dimitrie Ghica, its halls house several entomological collections from different areas of the world.

Museum für Naturkunde "Grigore Antipa"

Es wurde 1834 vom Fürsten Alessandro Dimitrie Ghica gegründet. In seinem Inneren befinden sich zahlreiche Insektensammlungen, die aus verschiedenen Teilen der Welt stammen.

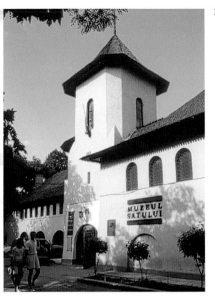

Satului Museum
15 hectares of land near Lake Herăstrău, where there are 298 examples of country village architecture.

Museum Satului
15 ha beim Herăstrăusee, wo sich 298 der verschiedensten Bauernhoftypen befinden.

1 Entry
2 Painted capital - Mărginimea Sibiului, 19th century
3 Wedding in Maramureşeană
4 House with verandah - Sibiu, 19th century
5 Women's peasant costume - Arad, 20th century

1 Eingang
2 Bemaltes Kapitell - Marginimea Sibiului, XIX. Jh.
3 Hochzeit in der Maramures
4 Haus mit Veranda - Sibiu, XIX. Jh.
5 Tracht einer Bäuerin - Arad, XX. Jh.

CERNICA MONASTERY

Cernica Monastery, ancient center of prayer and culture, was built, according to what Radu Voda Serban stated in his 1608 acts, by order of the Governor Cernica Stirbei. In that year, the Governor Cernica Serban decided to have the old monastery refurbished, surrounding it with fields, forests and villages and giving it his name, in memory of his family. Set in a quaint site near Bucharest, the monastery rises in the middle of a lake, surrounded by secular forests, attracting those who love nature as well as the worshippers.

Kloster Cernica, ein antikes religiöses Kulturzentrum, wurde, wie aus den Urkunden des Jahres 1608 von Radu Vodà Serban hervorgeht, durch den Gouverneur Cernica Stirbei gegründet. In jenem Jahr beschloß der Statthalter Cernica Serban eine alte Ein-siedelei wiederherzustellen, gab ihr seinen Namen, umgab sie mit Ländereien, Wäldern und Dörfern zum Andenken an seine Familie. In einem malerischen Ort in der Umgebung von Bukarest erhebt sich das Kloster inmitten eines Sees, von jahrhundertealten Wäldern umgeben, mit großer Anziehungskraft sowohl für Naturfreunde als auch für gläubige Christen.

1 Cernica monastery (1608)
2 Saint Lazarus Church (1804)
3 Saint Calinic of Cernica
4 Cover of the Gospels
5 Saint Calinic, patron saint of
   Cernica monastery
6 Refectory
7 Vault of the refectory

1 Kloster Cernica (1608)
2 Kirche St. Lazarus (1804)
3 San Calinic da Cernica
4 Bibelumschlag
5 Hl. Calinic, Schutzpatron des
   Klosters Cernica
6 Refektorium
7 Gewölbe des Refektoriums

Bucureşti-Mogoşoaia

The palace of Prince Constantine Brancovan (1702)

Palast des Fürsten Constantin Brancoveanu (1702)

Ploieşti

Important oil drilling and refinery center

Wichtiges Zentrum für Erdölgewinnung und Raffination

1 *Orthodox cathedral*
2 *Station*
3 *Center*

1 *Orthodoxe Kirche*
2 *Bahnhof*
3 *Stadtmitte*

SINAIA

1 View from the top of the
mountain (1400 m)
2 Casino
3 Typical villa
4 Center

1 Panorama vom Gipfel des
Berges aus (1400 m)
2 Kasino
3 Typische Villa
4 Stadtmitte

Sinaia
Sinaia Monastery
(1690-1695)

Inside is the largest museum of religious art in Romania, with a rich collection of icons.

Im Inneren befindet sich das bedeutendste Museum religiöser Kunst Rumäniens, mit einem reichen Bestand an Ikonen.

2 Detail of the door in Brancovan style
3 Interior of the church - Thrones
4-5-6-7 Icons

2 Detail des Portals im Brâncoveanustil
3 Das Innere der Kirche - Throne
4-5-6-7 Ikonen

SINAIA - VALEA PRAHOVEI

Peleş Castle, the stupendous summer residence of King Carol I of Romania.

Schloß Peleş, erhabene Sommer-residenz des Königs Karl I. von Rumänien.

1 *Side view of the castle*
2 *Carol I., king of Romania*
3 *Side view of the castle*
4 *Detail*

1 *Seitenansicht des Schlosses*
2 *Karl I., König von Rumänien*
3 *Seitenanblick des Schlosses*
4 *Detail*

VALEA PRAHOVEI

1 *Azuga area - Bucegi Mountains*
2 *Predeal, a winter ski resort with excellent facilities and a summer paradise for mountain lovers*
3 *Sunset over the Bucegi Mountains*

1 *Ortschaft Azuga - Bucegiberge*
2 *Predeal, ein vorzüglich ausgestattetes Winterskigebiet und Sommerparadies für Gebirgsliebhaber*
3 *Sonnenuntergang über den Bucegibergen*

BRAŞOV

One of the most beautiful medieval cities of Romania. Influenced by Saxon culture, it is the site of international singing competitions such as "Cerbul de Aur" and the stupendous, costumed popular festival with horses known as "Junii Braşovului." Only 20 km from Bran and about 20 km from Poiana Braşov, it is surrounded by dense forests.

Eine der schönsten mittelalterlichen Städte Rumäniens. Mit sächsischem Kultureinfluß ist es Sitz internationaler Singveranstaltungen, wie "Cerbul de Aur", und des reizvollen Volksfestes mit Trachten und Pferden "Junii Braşovului". Nur 20 km trennt es von Bran und auch die Entfernung von Poiana Braşov beträgt nur etwa 20 km. Es liegt inmitten von dichten Wäldern.

POIANA BRAŞOV

Only 20 km from Braşov is this pearl of Romania's winter and summer vacation areas.

Nur 20 km von Brasov entfernt befindet sich die Perle des Winter- und Sommerurlaubs Rumäniens.

1 The Cristianul Mare chalet
2 Hotel complex
3-4 Capra Neagră cable car

1 Die Hütte Cristianul Mare
2 Ein Hotelkomplex
3-4 Die Seilbahn Capra Neagră

3

4

THE MYSTERY OF BRAN'S CASTLE

Built in the Middle Ages, originally as a fortified customs station for an important commercial route, it was described in detail by the famous Venetian trader Pigafetta in his scrupulous diary.

The castle takes its name from the village in which it stands, which in its turn was named by its ancient residents, referring either to Bran, the mythological Celtic giant whose severed head rendered its owner oblivious to the passage of time and, when buried, protected the country from foreign aggressors, or to Bran, the mythological owner of "sacred time" that suspends the passing of "profane time."

What could be the connection between Bran and Dracula, the immortal vampire who lives by turning his victims into vampires?

It is said that in the Middle Ages there were wolf men in the forests of Transylvania who were reputed to be immortal, and who had long canine teeth and faces completely covered with hair. The bite of these creatures would infect and sicken their victims. For this reason, once they were killed by the populace, they were decapitated and buried face down.

In order to prevent them from resuscitating, stakes of ash wood were driven into their hearts from the back.

It seems that Prince Vlad Ţepeş Dracul, an enthusiastic military commander and exterminator of invaders, was himself infected by the bite of one of these creatures, as it is said that he used to drink the blood of his victims as a ritual to celebrate his victories. Indeed, a tomb attributed to him contained a decapitated body in a face down position. What mystery surrounds his burial and death? Entire families of these people with completely hair-covered faces are now scattered throughout the world. Are they the heirs of this species or just a curious joke of nature? Mystery? Legend? Whatever it may be, this marvelous castle awaits your visit.

1 Bran's castle, legendary residence of Count Dracula the vampire
2 Portrait of Prince Vlad Ţepeş the mythical Dracula
3 Little church of Queen Mary
4 Interior of the castle

30

DAS GEHEIMNIS DES SCHLOSSES VON BRAN

Ursprünglich im Mittelalter als befestigte Zollstelle einer wichtigen Handelsarterie entstanden, ist es ausgiebig vom bekannten venezianischen Kaufmann Pigafetta in seinem detaillierten Tagebuch beschrieben worden. Das Schloß wird nach dem Dorf benannt, in welchem es erbaut wurde und das seinerseits den Namen von den früheren Bewohnern erhielt: ....Bran, der mythologische keltische Riese, dessen vom Rumpf abgetrennter Kopf seinen Besitzer das Verfließen der Zeit vergessen läßt und der, wenn er begraben wird, das Land vor dem Eindringen von fremden Feinden schützt,......... oder Bran, der mythologische Inhaber der "heiligen Zeit", der die Dauer der "profanen Zeit" aufhebt. Welche Verbindung kann zwischen Bran und Dracula, dem Vampir, bestehen, der ewig lebt und sich reproduziert, indem er Blut aus seinen Opfern saugt? Man erzählt, daß im Mittelalter in den Wäldern Siebenbürgens Wolfsmenschen lebten, die als unsterblich galten, lange Eckzähne besaßen und deren Gesicht mit einem dichten Fell bedeckt war. Der Biß dieser Kreaturen infizierte die Opfer. Deshalb wurden sie von der Bevölkerung getötet und ohne Kopf bäuchlings begraben. Um zu verhindern, daß sie wieder auferstanden, wurde ihnen vom Rücken her ein Eschenholzstück ins Herz gestochen. Es hat den Anschein, daß Herzog Vlad Ţepeş Dracul, stürmischer Feldherr und Ausrotter von Eindringlingen, selbst von dieser Krankheit angesteckt worden war, denn man berichtet, er pflege das Blut seiner Opfer zu trinken, um seinen Sieg zu feiern. Welches Geheimnis umhüllt seinen Tod und seine Beerdigung, da man das ihm zugeschriebene Grab mit einem enthaupteten Körper in Bauchlage vorfand? Ganze Familien solcher Menschen mit vollständig behaarten Gesichtern sind noch überall auf der Welt verstreut. Sind sie die Erben dieser Spezies oder nur eine kuriose Laune der Natur? Geheimnis? Legende? Auf jeden Fall erwartet dieses wunderbare Schloß Ihren Besuch.

1 Das Schloß von Bran, die legendäre Residenz des Grafen Dracula, der Vampir
2 Porträt des Herzogs Vlad Ţepeş, der sagenhafte Dracula
3 Kleine Kirche der Königin Maria
4 Das Innere des Schlosses

3

4

1 Recently discovered secret
  passage
2 Conference room
3 Inner courtyard
4 16th century German chest
5 17th century Italian stool.
  Center: head of wolf man
6 Guard post

1 Ein vor kurzem entdeckter
  geheimer Gang
2 Ratssaal
3 Der Innenhof
4 Truhe aus dem XVI. Jh.,
  Deutschland
5 Hocker aus dem XVII. Jh.,
  Italien. In der Mitte: Kopf eines
  Wolfsmenschen
6 Wachposten

Castelul Râşnov

Râşnov Castle. About 10 km from Bran and 10 km from Brasov, it rises over the abandoned medieval town of Râsnov.

Schloß Râşnov. Etwa 10 km von Bran und 10 km von Kronstadt entfernt erhebt sich die verlassene Burg Râşnov.

FĂGĂRAŞ

The town of Făgăraşului (14th-17th century) was the residence of Prince Mihai Viteazu.

Burg Făgăraşului (XIV. - XVII. Jh.) war die Residenz des Fürsten Mihai Viteazu.

HUNEDOARA

Town of Prince Iaon of Hunedoara.

Burg des Fürsten Ioan di Hunedoara.

Corvin's Castle

Das Corvin-Schloß

SIBIU

Mediaeval city of Saxon cultural influence, it is an important center for tourism.

Es ist eine mittelalterliche Stadt sächsischen Kultureinflusses und wichtiges Touristenzentrum.

1 Sibiu by night
2-3 Orthodox cathedral
4 The masons' tower
   (16th century) - Old walls
5 Gothic style evangelical church
   (14th century)
6 Grand Square

1 Hermannstadt bei Nacht
2-3 Orthodoxe Kathedrale
4 Die Burg der Maurer (XVI. Jh.) -
   Alte Mauern
5 Evangelische Kirche im
   gotischen Stil (XIV. Jh.)
6 Großer Platz

SIGHIŞOARA

15th century city in Transylvania; this perfectly conserved city is the birthplace of Vlad Ţepeş (Dracula)

Die vollständig erhaltene Stadt des XV. Jahrhunderts in Sieben-bürgen ist die Geburtsstadt von Vlad Ţepeş (Dracula)

1 Panorama
2 Clock tower (1648)
3 The Romanian wolf, eternal testimony of the Latin origins of the Romanian people
4 The house in which Vlad Ţepeş (Dracula) was born
5 View

1 Panorama
2 Uhrturm (1648)
3 Die römische Wölfin ist ein ewiges Zeugnis des römischen Ursprungs des rumänischen Volkes
4 Geburtshaus von Vlad Ţepeş (Dracula)
5 Ansicht

TARGU MUREŞ
Transylvania

1 Orthodox cathedral
2 Prefecture palace

1 Orthodoxe Kathedrale
2 Palast der Präfektur

CLUJ - NAPOCA

This marvelous, industrious city in Transylvania (one of the great regions of Romania) was an ancient Roman fort known as Claustra Napoca. Recent archeological excavations show that today's city center was the center of the ancient city as well. The city has many museums, from open-air ethnographic exhibits to the Botanical Gardens, the history museum and the art museum. It is the birthplace of illustrious scientists, for example János Bolyai, the "Christopher Columbus" of mathematics.

Eine emsige, faszinierende Stadt Siebenbürgens (eine der großen Regionen Rumäniens), die antike römische Festung "Claustra Napoca" Die jüngsten archäologischen Ausgrabungen bezeugen, daß das Stadtzentrum von heute dasselbe von damals ist. Die Stadt ist Sitz vieler Museen, vom ethnographischen Museum im Freien zum Botanischen Garten, vom Geschichts- zum Kunstmuseum. Es ist die Geburtsstadt von berühmten Wissenschaftlern, wie zum Beispiel Janos Bolyai, der "Christophorus Kolumbus" der Mathematik.

1 Panorama
2 The Orthodox cathedral on Avram Iancu Square
3 The Romanian Post Office building
4 Unirii Square, with St. Michael's Roman Catholic cathedral

1 Panorama
2 Die orthodoxe Kathedrale auf dem Platz Avram Iancu
3 Der rumänische Postpalast
4 Uniriiplatz mit der römisch-katholischen Kirche St. Michael

ORADEA

City on the Hungarian border

Eine Stadt an der Grenze zu Ungarn

Night on the Crisul Repede river, with city hall in the background

Nachtansicht auf dem Fluß Crisul Repede, im Hintergrund das Rathaus

TIMIŞOARA

1 *Unirii Square*
2 *Victory Square and Orthodox cathedral*
3 *Unirii Square*

1 *Uniriiplatz*
2 *Platz des Sieges und orthodoxe Kathedrale*
3 *Uniriiplatz*

ARAD

Renowned for its textile and heavy mechanic industry.

Wichtiges Zentrum für Textilverarbeitung und Schwermechanik.

Avenue of the Revolution

Straße der Revolution

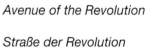

2

3

41

LUGOJ

This charming town on the western side of the country is the site of the "European Business School C.I. Dragan".

Dieses anmutige Städtchen im Westen des Landes ist Sitz der Universität "European Business School C.I. Dragan".

View along the Timiş river

Ansicht des Flusses Timiş

BĂILE HERCULANE

Thermal spa founded by the Romans, now the best known thermal baths in Europe.

Die von den Römern gegründeten Thermen gehören heute zu den bekanntesten Thermalortschaften Europas.

BĂILE GOVORA

Thermal baths for treating rheumatic complaints.

Thermen zur Behandlung von Rheumakrankheiten.

TARGU JIU

1 Monumental Ensemble
 (Constantin Brâncuşi)
 - The Silence Table
 - The Kiss Gate
 - Endless Column
2 Victory Street

1 Trigemenea (Constantin
 Brâncuşi
 - Die Tafel des Schweigens
 - Das Tor des Kusses
 - Säule ohne Ende
2 Siegesstraße

DROBETA-TURNU SEVERIN

3 Ruins of an abutment of the
 Trajan Bridge that once
 crossed the Danube, built by
 the architect Apollodor of
 Damascus (around 102-105)

3 Reste einer Brückenstütze der
 vom Architekten Apollodor von
 Damaskus erbauten
 "Trajansbrücke", die die Donau
 überquerte (ca. 102-105)

RÂMNICU VÂLCEA

Town on the Olt river, at the foot of the Transylvanian Alps. Point of departure to numerous thermal baths and monasteries.

Ortschaft am Fluß Alt, zu Füßen der Siebenbürger Alpen. Ausgangspunkt zu vielen Thermen und Klöstern.

BISTRIŢA MONASTERY (COSTESTI) 1492-1494

Holds the remains of Saint Gregory Decapolitul in a precious silver coffin. The inside murals were painted by Gheorghe Tătărăscu in 1855.

Hier werden die irdischen Reste des Heiligen Grigore Decapolitul in einem kostbaren Silbersarg aufbewahrt. Die inneren Wandmalereien stammen vom Maler Gheorghe Tătărăscu aus dem Jahre 1855.

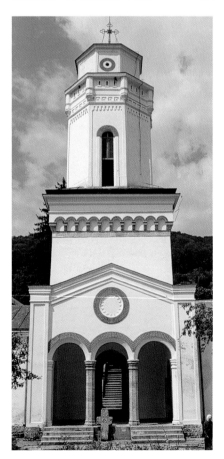

44

CRAIOVA

Ancient fort of the Dacians known as Pelendava, now one of the most important cities in Romania. It is an industrial area for the construction of machinery and locomotives, and continues in its role as pilot center for the national economy. Here are Bibescu Park, the art museum, and the opera theater. The inventor of the fountain pen, Petrache Poenaru (1799-1875), is a native of Craiova.

Antike Dakerfestung mit dem Namen Pelendava, heute eine der wichtigsten Städte Rumäniens. Industriesitz für Automobil- und Lokomotivherstellung, verteidigt seine Rolle als Führungszentrum der nationalen Wirtschaft. Hier finden wir den Bibescupark, das Kunstmuseum, das Operntheater. Aus Craiova gebürtig ist der Erfinder des Füllfederhalters Petrache Poenaru (1799 - 1875).

PITEŞTI

This important Romanian industrial city, site of the Dacia automobile factory, is a major center oil drilling and refinery center.
It is connected to the capital by the Piteşti-Bucharest highway.

Wichtige rumänische Industriestadt, Sitz der Autofabrik "Dacia" und bedeutendes Zentrum zur Gewinnung und Raffination von Erdöl. Mit der Hauptstadt durch die Autobahn Piteşti-Bukarest verbunden.

CURTEA DE ARGEŞ MONASTERY

Built by Prince Neagoe Basarab in 1517 on the site of an earlier church, and site of the first Mitropolia of Wallachia, built by Vlad Ţepeş in the 15th century. Inside are the tombs of donors Neagoe Basarab and Despina Doamna, as well as that of Prince Radu de la Afumaţi. The tombs of the first kings of Romania, Carol I and Ferdinand, with Queens Elizabeth and Mary, are also here. It is currently the residence of the Episcopal Palace of Argeşului and holds the remains of Saint Philophthea.

Im Jahre 1517 vom Fürsten Neagoe Basarab an der Stelle einer früheren Kirche errichtet, erster Metropolitensitz der Walachei, der von Vlad Ţepeş im XV. Jh. erbaut wurde.
Im Inneren befinden sich die Grabmäler der Spender Neagoe Basarab und Despina Doamna, sowie des Fürsten Radu de la Afumaţi. Auch finden wir hier die Gräber der ersten rumänischen Könige, Karl I. und Ferdinand mit den Königinnen Elisabeth und Maria. Jetzt ist es Sitz des Bischofs von Argeşului. Hier sind die Gebeine der hl. Filofteia aufgebahrt.

DINTR-UN LEMN MONASTERY (1635) FRÂNCEȘTI COMMUNITY

Inside the church are the tombs of the wife and son of Prince Șerban Cantacuzino. The monastery contains a priceless collection of art, especially wooden icons.

Hier befinden sich die Grabmäler der Frau und des Sohns des Fürsten Șerban Cantacuzino. Das Kloster beherbergt eine unschätzbare Sammlung von Kunstgegenständen, hauptsächlich Holzikonen.

TISMANA MONASTERY (1377-1378) TISMANA COMMUNITY

Built in Romanesque style with neo-Gothic elements, and immersed in dense vegetation. Inside are precious works of art and religious objects.

Ein mitten im Grünen liegendes Bauwerk im romanischen Stil mit neugotischen Elementen. Im Inneren befinden sich bedeutende Kunst- und Kultgegenstände.

HOREZU MONASTERY
(1690-1694)

The largest medieval architecture complex in Wallachia. The monastery's art collection includes a photography museum and a rich treasure of icons and Brancovan silver. The monastery also has a library with over 4500 volumes.

Der größte Komplex von mittelalterlicher Architektur in der Walachei. Die Kunstsammlung des Klosters umfaßt ein Fotomuseum und einen reichhaltigen Schatz an Ikonen und "Brâncoveanu" Silberwaren. Ferner besitzt das Museum eine Bibliothek mit über 4500 Bänden.

1 Principality
2 Stelea church
3 Chindiei Tower
4 Mitropolita basilica

1 Fürstentum
2 Steleakirche
3 Chindieiturm
4 Metropolitenbasilika

DEALU MONASTERY
TÂRGOVIŞTE

Located on the top of a hill that overlooks Târgovişte, the monastery holds the relics of princes and mercenary leaders. Here are buried the heads of Mihai Viteazu, Radu Cel Mare, Pătraşcu Cel Bun, Vladislav II, and Mihai Movilă. It has a history and art museum.

Auf der Spitze eines Hügels, der Târgovişte überragt, beherbergt das Kloster die Reliquien von Fürsten und Feldherrn. Hier sind der Kopf von Mihai Viteazu, Radu Cel Mare, Pătraşcu Cel Bun, Wladislaw II. und Mihail Movilă bestattet. Es besitzt ein Geschichts- und Kunstmuseum.

CONSTANTA -TOMIS

Founded by the Greeks in the 6th century BCE, it was later colonized by the Romans. Countless archeological finds testify to the historic past of this ancient city. It is Romania's main port on the Black Sea and contains an archeology museum, natural history museum, the Romanian Navy museum, ethnographic and natural science museums, dolphin tanks and the aquarium.

Von den Griechen im VI. Jh. v.Chr. errichtet, wurde es später von den Römern kolonisiert. Zahlreiche archäologische Funde zeugen von der geschichtlichen Vergangenheit dieser überaus alten Stadt. Haupthafen Rumäniens am Schwarzen Meer, gibt es hier ein archäologisches und ein naturwissenschaftliches Museum, sowie das Museum der rumänischen Marine, das für Naturkunde, das Delphinarium und Aquarium.

1 Panorama
2 Mosque
3 Orthodox archiepiscopal
   cathedral

1 Panorama
2 Moschee
3 Erzbischöfliche orthodoxe
   Kathedrale

1

2

3

CONSTANTA - TOMIS

1 Casino
2 Archeological finds
3 Center
4 Archeological museum on Ovid
   Square

1 Kasino
2 Archäologische Funde
3 Stadtzentrum
4 Archäologisches Museum auf
   dem Ovidplatz

NĂVODARI

Children's summer camp
Ferienkolonie für Kinder

SF. MONASTERY
TECHIRGHIOL

Little wooden church brought
here from Ardeal
Altar inside the church

Kleine, von Ardeal hierher verlegte
Holzkirche
Altar im Inneren der Kirche

THE BLACK SEA COAST
DIE SCHWARZMEERKÜSTE

1 Constance - Mamaia - Beach
2 Hotel Onix with sulfur pool
3 Panorama of the coast
4 Local crafts
5 Olimp beach center
6 Eforie
7 Lake Constance
8 Panorama

1 Kontanza - Mamaia - Strand
2 Hotel Onix mit
  Schwefelschwimmbad
3 Panorama der Küste
4 Lokales Handwerk
5 Strand des Olimpkomplexes
6 Eforie
7 Kontanzasee
8 Panorama

4

5

1

6

7

8

HISTRIA

Archeological site with Greco-Roman finds from the 7th century BCE

Archäologischer Komplex mit griechisch-römischen Funden aus dem VII. Jh. v.Chr.

HERACLEA - CETĂŢUIA

1 Fortified Byzantine city of Enisala

1 Die ausgebaute byzantinische Festung Enisala

TULCEA

2 Important port on the Danube, departure point for excursions to the delta.
3 Port
4 Monument to Independence (1899)

2 Wichtiger Donauhafen, Ausgangsbasis für Ausflüge ins Delta
3 Hafen
4 Unabhängigkeitsdenkmal (1899)

3 4

DANUBE DELTA

With its source in the Black Forest of Germany, the Danube flows all the way to the Black Sea, creating a true natural paradise 5165 square kilometers in size. The Danube Delta is an ecosystem that offers shelter to more than 300 species of birds, flora and fauna which proliferate in this incredible natural oasis.

DONAUDELTA

Die Donau entspringt im Schwarzwald in Deutschland und mündet ins Schwarze Meer, wobei sie ein wahrhaftes Natur-paradies mit 5165 km2 bildet. Das Donaudelta ist ein Ökosystem, das mehr als 300 Arten von Vögeln, Flora und Fauna Zuflucht bietet, die sich in dieser unwahr-scheinlichen Naturoase reichlich vermehren können.

BRĂILA

Important river port on the Danube.

Wichtiger Binnenhafen an der Donau.

1 Panorama of the Danube
2 Independence Square
3 Trajan Square - Blue Clock

1 Panorama auf die Donau
2 Platz der Unabhängigkeit
3 Trajansplatz - Blaue Uhr

GALATI

Duty-free area on the Danube.

Zollfreizone an der Donau.

1 St. Precista church (1647)
2 Center
3 History Museum
4 Park
5 Tourist harbor

1 Wehrkirche Precista (1647)
2 Stadtzentrum
3 Geschichtsmuseum
4 Park
5 Touristenhafen

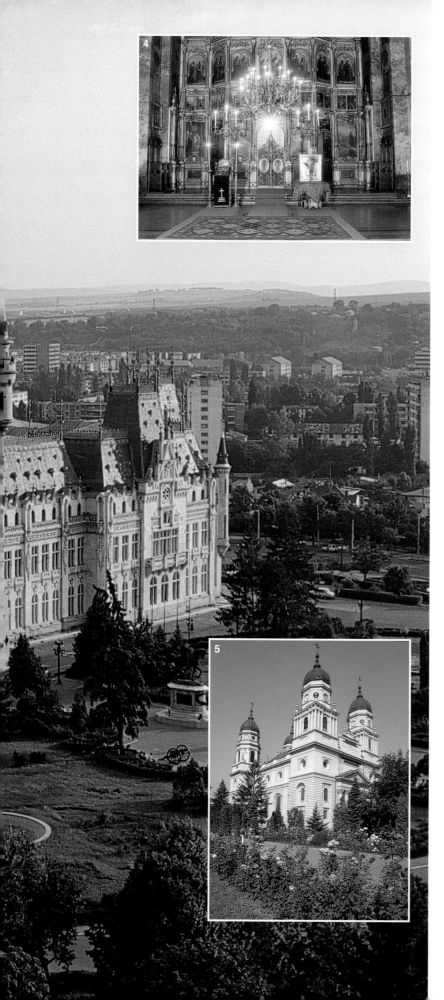

IAŞI

Cultural capital of Romania, a true open-air museum. The city is the birthplace of poets, writers, musicians and artists in general: Mihai Eminescu, Ion Creanga, Nicolae Iorga, A.I. Cuza, Vasile Alexandri, Mihail Kogălniceanu, Ciprian Porumbescu and countless others. Famous for its churches (Trei Ierarhi, Cetăţuia and Golia), Iaşul is home to the Mitropolia of Moldavia and Bucovina, numerous museums, and the Copou Botanical Gardens (20,000 species of flowers), and the nearby forests and its famous wines are only some of the attractions offered. Conscious of its noble origins, the city has numerous monuments to its most important hero, the Prince of Moldavia Stefan Cel Mare (1457-1504).

Kulturelle Hauptstadt Rumäniens, ein wahres Freilichtmuseum. In der Stadt stand die Wiege von Dichtern, Schriftstellern, Musikern und Künstlern im allgemeinen: Mihai Eminescu, Ion Creanga, Nicolae Iorga, A.I. Cuza, Vasile Alexandri, Mihail Kogălniceanu, Ciprian Porumbescu und viele mehr. Berühmt wegen seiner Kirchen (Trei Ierarhi, Cetăţuia, Golia), befindet sich in Jassy der Sitz des Metropoliten der Moldau und der Bukowina. Zahlreiche Museen, der Botanische Garten Copou (20.000 Blumenarten), die nahen Wälder und die bekannten Weine sind nur einige der anziehenden Angebote. Sich seines edlen Ursprungs bewußt, bewahrt die Stadt jederzeit ein gutes Andenken an ihren wichtigsten Helden, den Moldaufürst Stephan den Großen (1457 - 1504).

1 *The Culture Palace (1906-1925) in Flamboy neo-Gothic style, contains the art, history, ethnography and polytechnic museums*
2 *National Theater*
3 *The relics of St. Paraschiva, the protector of Moldavia*
4 *Mitropolitana cathedral - Interior - Altar*
5 *Mitropolitana cathedral*

1 *Kulturpalast (1908 - 1925) im neugotischen Flamboystil und Sitz von 4 Museen : Kunst- und Geschichtsmuseum, das ethnographische Museum und das Polytechnikum*
2 *Nationaltheater*
3 *Die Reliquien der hl. Paraschiva, Beschützerin der Moldau*
4 *Metropolitenkirche - Das Innere - Altar*
5 *Metropolitenkirche*

67

IAŞI

1 The Trei Ierarhi church
2 Interior
3 Golia Monastery

1 Die Kirche Trei Ierarhi
2 Das Innere
3 Kloster Golia

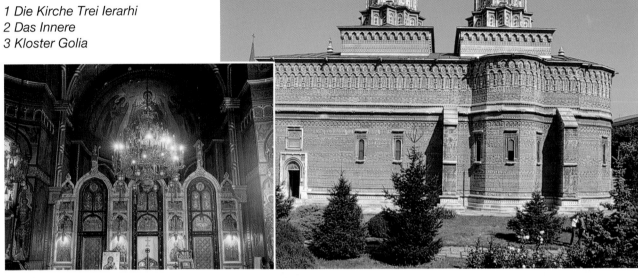

CETĂŢUIA MONASTERY

The monastery complex is protected by strong walls 1.40 meters thick and about 7 meters high. The monastery has a rich collection of art objects, on display in an elegant museum.

Der Klosterkomplex ist von mächtigen Mauern umgeben, die 1,40 m tief und etwa 7 m hoch sind. In ihm befindet sich eine reiche Sammlung von Kunstgegenständen, die in einem eleganten Museum ausgestellt ist.

4-5 Cetăţuia monastery
6-7 Museum of the Cetăţuia
  monastery

4-5 Kloster Cetăţuia
6-7 Museum des Klosters Cetăţuia

BOTOŞANI

North-western city, where the textile industry is flourishing.

Stadt im Nordosten des Landes mit blühender Texilindustrie.

DOROHOI

Famous glass industry center.

Bekanntes Zentrum für Glasherstellung.

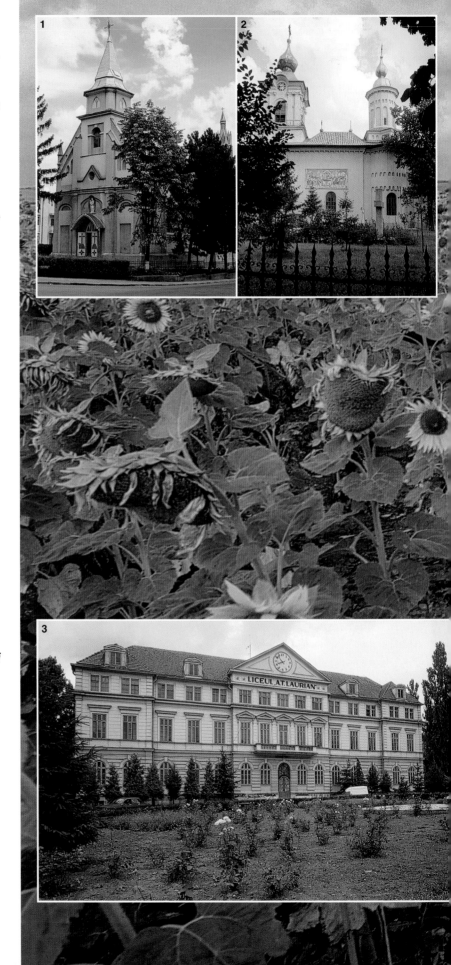

1 St. Joseph's Catholic church
2 Orthodox church of St. Nicholas
3 A.T. Laurian high school
4 DOROHOI - Father Dumitru Furtună - great man of letters and patron - symbol of great national spirituality
5 Ipoteşti - Bust of the poet Mihai Eminescu
6 Ipoteşti - House of Mihai Eminescu

1 Katholische Josephskirche
2 Orthodoxe Nikolauskirche
3 A.T. Laurian Gymnasium
4 DOROHOI - Pater Dumitru Furtună - großer Literat und Mäzen - Symbol der tiefen nationalen Geistigkeit
5 Ipoteşt - Büste des Dichters Mihai Eminescu
6 Ipoteşti - Haus von Mihai Eminescu

SUCEAVA

1 Old city of Suceava (1388)

2-3 Church of St. George (1514-1522). Inside is the silver coffin with the relics of St. John the New. Brought to Suceava in 1402 by Alexander the Good, they were transferred to this church by Peter the Lame in 1589.

4-5-6 Neamţ monastery - Panorama, entry and miraculous icon of the Madonna (1402)

7 Buffalo

1 Antike Festung Suceava (1388)

2-3 Georgskirche (1514 - 1522), im Inneren befindet sich der Silbersarg mit den Reliquien des hl. Johannes dem Neuen. Sie wurden 1402 von Alexander dem Guten nach Suceava gebracht und 1589 von Peter dem Lahmen in diese Kirche verlegt.

4-5-6 Kloster Neamţ. Panorama, Eingang und wundertätige Ikone der Madonna (1402)

7 Wisent

VORONEŢ MONASTERY

The "Sistine Chapel" of the East, it was donated by Stefan the Great in 1488, and the outside was painted in 1550 with the famous "Voroneţ Blue."

Die "Sixtinische Kapelle" des Ostens wurde von Stephan dem Großen 1488 gestiftet und 1550 außen mit dem berühmten "Voroneţer Blau" bemalt.

NEAMŢ MONASTERY (14TH CENTURY)

Center of calligraphers and illuminators, it has a rich collection of religious art, wooden sculptures and the miraculous icon of the Madonna, known as "the flying icon" (1402). It has a good library (about 1800 volumes and manuscripts).
Not far away is the park, a natural reserve ruled by the buffalo, a powerful symbol of this land.

Zentrum von Kalligraphen und Miniaturmalern, besitzt es eine wertvolle Sammlung von religiösen Kunstgegenständen, Holzskulpturen und die wundertätige Ikone der Madonna, "die fliegende Ikone" (1402). Es gibt eine reiche Bibliothek (etwa 1800 Werke und Manuskripte).
Nicht weit von hier befindet sich ein Park, eine natürliche Reserve, wo der Wisent der Hauptdarsteller ist, das mächtige Symbol dieser Gegend.

SECU MONASTERY (1602)

This fortified monastery contains a rich museum of religious art of great historical interest.

Eine Klosterfestung, im Inneren befindet sich ein reichhaltiges Museum für kirchliche Kunst von großer geschichtlicher Bedeutung.

VĂRATEC MONASTERY (1785)

Originally built of wood (1785), it combines traditional Moldavian elements with those of Neoclassicism. Its extraordinary beauty makes it quite popular.

Ursprünglich aus Holz (1785), vereinigt es traditionelle Moldau-elemente mit neuklassizistischen. Wegen seiner außerordentlichen Schönheit viel besucht.

AGAPIA MONASTERY
(1642)

Totally rebuilt in 1858-1862, its interior is painted by Nicolae Grigorescu. It has a library of 17,000 volumes and a rich museum of religious art.

Von 1858 - 1862 radikal umgebaut, ist es im Inneren von Nicolae Grigorescu bemalt, besitzt eine Bibliothek mit 17.000 Bänden und ein reiches Museum mit Werken kirchlicher Kunst.

SIHĂSTRIA MONASTERY
(1740)

The original wooden church was built in 1740. The present-day church, made of river rock and brick, is dated 1724. It contains icons painted by the famous monk and painter Tătărăscu.

Die erste Kirche wurde 1740 aus Holz errichtet. Die heutige, aus Fluß- und Ziegelstein, stammt aus dem Jahre 1824. Hier befinden sich die vom berühmten Mönch-Maler Tătărăscu bemalten Ikonen.

BISTRITA MONASTERY
VIIŞOARA COMMUNITY

Fortified monastery near the city of Piatra Neamt, built in various stages with the aid of four donations. Inside the church is the miraculous icon of St. Anne, presented to the wife of Alexander the Good by one of the last Byzantine empresses from the Paleologi family (15th century).

Ein befestigtes Kloster in der Nähe der Stadt Piatra Neamt, das in mehreren Etappen und dank vier Schenkungen erbaut wurde. Im Inneren wird die wundertätige Ikone der hl. Anna aufbewahrt, die der Frau Alexander des Guten von einer der letzten byzantinischen Kaiserinnen der Familie Paleologi (XV. Jh.) geschenkt wurde.

PIATRA NEAMŢ

1 House of Culture
2 Theater
3 Panorama

1 Kulturhaus
2 Theater
3 Panorama

CĂLUGĂRENI

The area is famous for the 1595 victory of the valiant Roman army, led by Mihai Viteazu, over the Turks.

Berühmt wegen des im Jahre 1595 durch die rumänischen Streitkräfte unter Mihai Viteazu errungenen Sieges über die Türken.

1 Monument to Mihai Viteazu
2 The village church
3 Memorial cross
   commemorating the battle of
   Călugăreni in 1595
4 Commemorative monument
5 The battlefield

1 Denkmal zu Ehren Mihai Viteazu
2 Die Dorfkirche
3 Gedenkkreuz an die Schlacht
   von Călugăreni im Jahre 1595
4 Denkmal
5 Das Schlachtfeld

GIURGIU

City on the Bulgarian border.
Here the border is marked by the Danube. Home of important shipyards.

Grenzstadt zu Bulgarien.
Hier bildet die Donau die Grenze.
Sitz von bedeutenden Schiffs-werften.

1 River terminal
2 Center
3 Ruins of the ancient fortress

1 Flußhafen
2 Stadtzentrum
3 Überreste der alten Festung

INDEX - INHALTSVERZEIHNIS

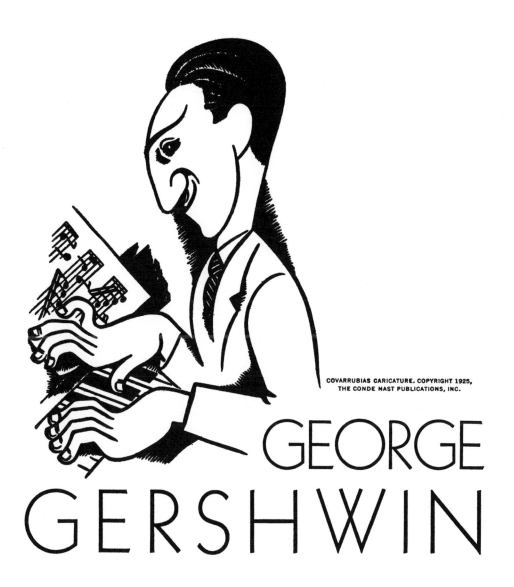

COVARRUBIAS CARICATURE. COPYRIGHT 1925,
THE CONDE NAST PUBLICATIONS, INC.

GEORGE
GERSHWIN

TO IRA